3 1865 00183 7755

W9-AQE-466

21.‑

RIVER FOREST PUBLIC LIBRARY
735 Lathrop Avenue
River Forest, Illinois 60305
708 / 366-5205

12/07

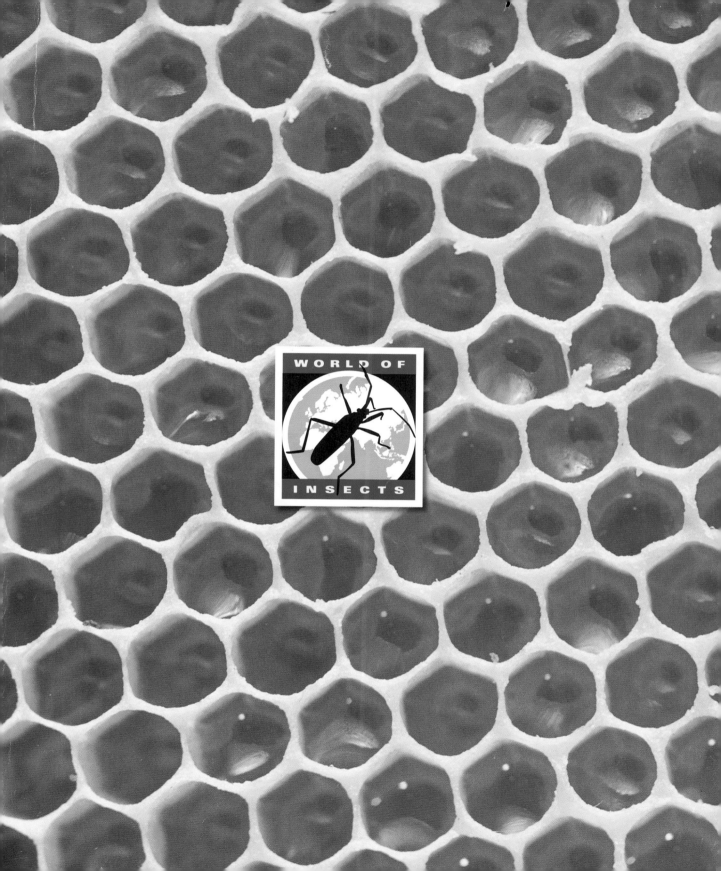

WORLD OF INSECTS

BEES

by Sophie Lockwood

Content Adviser: *Michael Breed, Ph.D., Professor,*
Ecology and Evolutionary Biology,
The University of Colorado, Boulder

RIVER FOREST PUBLIC LIBRARY
735 LATHROP
RIVER FOREST, IL 60305

THE CHILD'S WORLD®, MANKATO, MINNESOTA

Bees

Published in the United States of America by The Child's World®
1980 Lookout Drive • Mankato, MN 56003-1705
800-599-READ • www.childsworld.com

Acknowledgements:

The Child's World®: Mary Berendes, Publishing Director

The Creative Spark: Mary Francis, Project Director; Wendy Mead, Editor; Deborah Goodsite, Photo Researcher

The Design Lab: Kathleen Petelinsek, Designer and Production Artist

Photos:

Cover: Anthony Bannister/Gallo Images; frontispiece and CIP: Comstock; half title: Anthony Bannister/Gallo Images

Interior: Animals Animals: 11 (Patti Murray), 21 (Donald Specker); Corbis: 30 (Lynda Richardson); Istockphoto.com: 12 (Nicholas Homrich), 5, 29 (Malcolm Romain); Minden Pictures: 5, 24 (Michael Durham), 18 (Kim Taylor/npl),; Mira.com: 23 (Phil Degginger); Photo Researchers, Inc.: 5, 8, 16, 34 (Scott Camazine), 26 (John M. Coffman), 5, 33 (USDA/Nature Source), 36 (Darwin Dale); Visuals Unlimited: 5, 14 (Gary Meszaros).

Illustration: Kathleen Petelinsek: 7.

Library of Congress Cataloging-in-Publication Data

Lockwood, Sophie.
  Bees / by Sophie Lockwood.
    p. cm.—(The world of insects)
  Includes index.
  ISBN-13: 978-1-59296-818-3 (library bound: alk. paper)
  ISBN-10: 1-59296-818-X (library bound: alk. paper)
  1. Bees—Juvenile literature. I. Title.
  QL565.2.L63 2007
  595.79'9—dc22   2006103453

Copyright © 2008 by The Child's World®. All rights reserved. No part of the book may be reproduced or utilized in any form or by any means without written permission from the publisher.

TABLE OF CONTENTS

Chapter One

The Bee Waggle Dance

A worker honeybee steps in a half circle, then waggles and buzzes along a straight line. The honeybee turns, forming another half circle in the other direction. This figure-eight pattern is repeated several times as other workers touch the dancer with their **antennae**. Step right . . . step . . . step . . . waggle . . . waggle . . . No, this is not an insect version of the hokey-pokey. It is a message sent in honeybee Morse code: Look for nectar-rich flowers 200 meters (656 feet) to the left, at a right angle to the sun.

Only honeybees transmit this type of message about where to find food. A worker honeybee that finds a field of flowers needs to tell other workers where it is—which direction and how far. The forager needs other workers to help it collect the nectar and

Did You Know?
Candles made from honeybee beeswax smell like honey as they burn. Other products made from beeswax include furniture polish, lip balm, hand cream, and coatings for such candies as jelly beans.

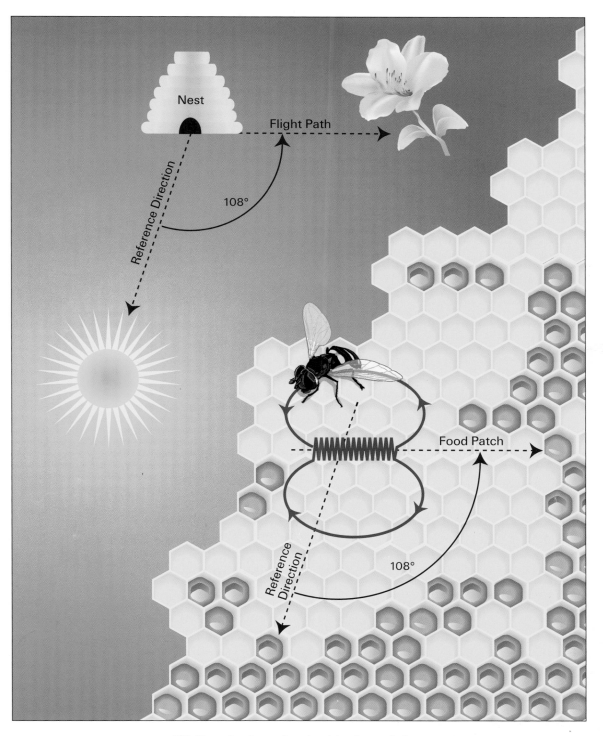

Nest

Flight Path

Reference Direction

108°

Food Patch

Reference Direction

108°

This illustration shows a honeybee doing the waggle dance.

pollen the flowers provide. The workers smell the scent of the flowers on the dancer and become excited.

For a food source up to about 50 meters (164 feet) away, the forager dances in a quick circle. The bee changes direction frequently—the more changes, the higher the calorie content of the food source. The round dance, as it is called, finds the bee moving clockwise, then counterclockwise, but always in a circle.

Would You Believe?
If twelve honeybees work together for all four weeks of their lives, they will produce 1 teaspoon of honey.

A honeybee dances to tell other bees where to find food.

Would You Believe?
A foraging worker honeybee performs a waggle run lasting 2.5 seconds to get help collecting nectar from a food source located about 2,625 meters (8,612 feet) from the hive.

For sources of food between 50 and 150 meters (164 and 492 feet) away, worker honeybees do the sickle dance. This dance involves a crescent-shaped pattern. It has elements similar to the round dance and the waggle dance and is used for signaling food at an in-between distance.

The waggle dance is used for food sources far from the hive. The worker honeybee lines up on the honeycomb and begins its dance. If the food source is directly toward the sun, the dance will be done vertically. If the food source is 45 degrees left of the sun, the worker will dance at a 45-degree angle left of vertical.

The length of time the honeybee waggles its **abdomen**, measured in seconds, indicates the distance from the hive to the food source. In addition to waggling, the worker honeybee makes a buzzing noise by flapping its wings quickly. The loud buzzing may be part of the message, a form of communication. Scientists do not know. What they do know is that this clever dancing makes nectar and pollen collecting a very efficient process.

Chapter Two

The Bee Cycle of Life

When most people think about bees, they think of honey and bee stings. There are about 25,000 species of bees. Only a few produce honey, but almost all can sting. For bees, stinging is one of their most important defenses. But for some bees, it is also a death sentence. There are about dozen or so types of honeybees that die after they sting. Some bees can protect themselves by biting or spraying chemicals.

Bees fall into two types: social bees and **solitary** bees. Social bees—types of honeybees, bumblebees, sweat bees, and others—live in colonies, and each colony has a queen to produce more worker bees. They build hives, work together, and depend on each other to survive.

Solitary bees are just what the name implies. They live by themselves. Females find a hole in a log or a crack in a wall and lay their eggs. They do not have workers available

to feed the young. For carpenter bees, mason bees, and leafcutter bees, solitary life is normal. Surprisingly, there are more species of solitary bees than social bees.

Many bees, such as this digger bee, live a solitary life.

head

thorax

abdomen

A BEE'S BODY

Bees, like other insects, have three-part bodies and six legs. Bees, close relatives of ants and wasps, have a complex head, a muscular **thorax**, and an abdomen.

A bee's body has three main sections: the head, the thorax, and the abdomen.

A bee's head is small, but very complicated. The most outstanding features are the eyes. Bees have two multi-faceted eyes with up to 12,000 separate **facets** called **ommatidia**. In between these compound eyes are three smaller simple eyes—called **ocelli**—that sense levels of light. Bees do not see like humans do. They cannot focus their eyes on specific items. They do, however, see motion, shape, and color.

Two antennae sit at the front of the face. Antennae serve as sense organs. They help the bee communicate with other bees. Just below the antennae is the mouth, made up of **mandibles**, or jaws, and a tongue that allows the bee to lap up or suck liquids, such as nectar.

The thorax is the central portion of the body. Both sets of wings attach to the thorax. Beneath the outer shell, or exoskeleton, lie muscles that coordinate flight. Each set of wings is transparent, and the front and hind wings work together. When a bee flies, the front and hind wings are attached with tiny hooks that work like Velcro® closures.

The legs also function in pairs. The front legs are used to clean the head, eyes, and mouthparts, all of which get coated with pollen. The middle legs clean the body and wings and remove pollen from

Did You Know?
Bees won't fly when the wind blows more than 25 kilometers per hour (15 miles per hour).

the pollen baskets on the rear legs. Honeybees also handle bits of wax, produced by worker bees from glands in the abdomen. The rear legs are primarily used to collect pollen. Sticky pollen clings to the long hairs on the ends of the rear legs.

Did You Know?
The total weight of the eggs laid in one day by a queen honeybee is more than she weighs.

A honeybee pollinates a rose.

The abdomen holds the major body systems: digestive organs, **reproductive** organs, and waste-disposal organs. It also contains the stinger for many bees. The stinger is located at the end of the abdomen and has a sac of venom attached to it. When a bee stings, it can continue to pump venom into its victim as long as the stinger remains intact.

REPRODUCTION

During its cycle of life, a bee undergoes a complete **metamorphosis**—a change from one body form to another. The change is similar to the change a butterfly goes through when going from caterpillar to adult.

A queen honeybee mates once in her life, and that mating will **fertilize** the many eggs she may lay in her lifetime. The eggs are tiny—only 1.2 millimeters (0.05 inches) long, or about the size of half a grain of rice. The queen lays the eggs in individual cells. For honeybees, a queen may lay as many as 1,900 eggs a day. Some solitary bees may lay as few as one egg a day, and ten or less during their lifetime.

The honeybee eggs hatch on day three, and pale, wormlike **larvae** crawl out. In a hive, the workers feed the larvae bee milk and bee bread (a mixture of honey,

pollen, and fluid). Worker bees pay their young charges a great deal of attention, visiting each larva as often as 1,300 times a day. In some solitary bees, the female lays her eggs on a mound of bee bread, which allows them to feed and grow with little attention. The larvae have one job: eat, eat, eat. As they grow, they pass through five stages called instars. During the last stage, the larva spins a cocoon, much like a moth does.

In the cocoon, the larva pupates into an adult bee. Wings, a furry or sleek body, and all the other aspects that make up a bee are present in the larva, just in a different

The cells inside this hive show honeybee eggs and larvae at different stages of development.

form. Chemical changes cause the larva to go through a complete body transformation. This entire process, from egg to adult, takes between two and three weeks. The length of time the process takes depends on the type of bee and the conditions within the hive or nest.

Solitary bees, such as mason bees, follow the same reproductive pattern, but they do not live in a hive. The female bee finds a hole in wood. She lines it with nectar, lays her egg, and seals the hole. She repeats this process once or twice daily during her one month of adult life.

WHAT ARE THE CHANCES?

From egg to adult, the chances of survival for most bee species are quite good. When scientists studied the lives of bumblebees, they discovered that just under half of all eggs survive to become adults. This is remarkably high when compared to butterflies, which have a survival rate of only one or two per hundred eggs.

Even with a high rate of survival, predators abound in nature. Spiders, wasps, ants, and mites feast on bee eggs and larvae. Hoverflies lay their eggs in bee nests, and their larvae enjoy a safe nursery environment in which to grow.

Several bird species—shrikes, bee-eaters, and flycatchers, for example—have learned how to remove stingers

before eating adult bees. Badgers, foxes, minks, and skunks happily uncover a bee's nest and eat the larvae. Of course, the mammal best known for robbing hives is the bear. Bears love honey, but they also eat bee eggs and larvae. A few stings on the nose are worth it if a hungry bear can fill its stomach with rich protein and delicious honey.

A leafcutter bee will use leaves to make a nest for its eggs. Here is a leafcutter bee larva.

Chapter Three

A Swarm of Bees

Some bees make honey, but most bees do not. Nearly all bees can sting, but some social bees, such as the tropical stingless bees, have other ways of protecting themselves. Some bees live in colonies, while others prefer a solitary life. Bees come in large, gawky shapes, like bumblebees. They can be slim and swift, like digger bees. Bees can be as small as 2 millimeters (0.08 inches) long or as large as 40 millimeters (1.6 inches) in length. As for colors, bees can be bright yellow, red, metallic green, shiny blue, or glistening black, with or without fuzzy bodies.

What nearly all bees do have in common is that they depend on pollen and flower nectar or oils for food sources. Because feeding depends on flowers, bees have become the most important **pollinating** insects. As bees hunt for nectar, they pick up pollen on their bodies that is later deposited on other flowers. Bees can be found on every continent except Antarctica and in every region except high mountains, polar areas, and a handful of small oceanic islands.

Social bees fall into three categories within the hive: workers, drones, or queens. The female social bees can be either queens or workers. In nearly all bee species, there is only one queen in a colony. At certain times of the year males, or drones, are also found in the nest, but they do not work in the colony.

The worker bees live for about four weeks, advancing from job to job as they age. In the beginning, workers perform janitor duties in the hive, repairing cells and cleaning. As they age, they become nursemaids to the larvae or the queen, and finally, they forage for food. Drones have only one job: mating. Once they have mated with a queen, they die. A queen honeybee mates once in her life with several drones, and then she becomes an egg-laying machine. A queen can control the sex of her offspring. She will lay mostly female worker eggs, only producing drones and possible new queens toward the end of her life. A queen honeybee may live as long as three to five years. Bumblebee and sweat bee queens live for only one season.

Solitary bees are different. They have many females capable of laying eggs. A female finds a nesting site and provides it with food (bee bread and honey). She lays her eggs on the food supply and may or may not tend her young, depending on the species of bee. Her young will be

both male and female, since they must mate and produce young themselves.

BEE FAMILIES

The largest and perhaps most interesting honeybee can be found in the foothills of the Himalaya Mountains. Avid builders, Asian honeybees construct a single honeycomb that can span 3 meters (10 feet). The comb hangs from a

A queen honeybee (center) mates once in her life.

Beware of Killer Bees

The big news in bees is the development of Africanized, or "killer," bees. The threat of attacks by these aggressive, easily annoyed bees has been discussed on television news programs and in newspapers and magazines.

Killer bees are not the result of a mad scientist working to create some type of super bee. In 1956, Brazilian scientists hoped to breed a new type of honeybee that would produce more honey and wax. They tried to mate wild African honeybees with domesticated Brazilian honeybees. What they got was a huge mistake: the Africanized, or killer, bee.

The African bees escaped from the labs and sneaked into hives of wild honeybees. The new bees are more aggressive than wild honeybees, but they produce less honey and less wax than normal domesticated honeybees. Just about anything annoys killer bees—loud noises, strong odors, shiny jewelry, or sudden motions. The bees consider anyone within 30 meters (100 feet) of their hive as a threat that they will chase for up to 400 meters (about 0.25 mile).

Sometimes killer bees sneak into a hive and dominate the honeybees already living there. As killer-bee queens begin laying eggs, the species takes over the normal hive activities. The killer bees also reproduce faster than normal bees. The killer bees have already moved northward through Central America and are now in Texas and other southern states.

high tree branch or the top of a cliff. The bees gather on the outside of the honeycomb in thick layers of living bees. On the lookout for danger, these bees fiercely guard their hive.

Honeybees swarm the outside of their hive to protect it.

When a worker detects a threat, it stings and also releases a **pheromone**. The pheromone signals danger. Picking up the scent, other workers swarm and attack the threat. This is a very effective means of protection, since such an attack by hundreds of angry bees can kill the invader.

Bumblebees are also social bees, or hive dwellers. Their communities are much smaller than honeybee colonies, with usually 30 to 400 bees per hive. Bumblebee colonies only survive during warm seasons. At summer's end, a new queen will mate and then **hibernate**, waiting for spring and the opportunity to start a new colony. The miracle of bumblebees is that they can fly at all. According to the laws of physics, their bodies are far too heavy and

Bumblebees collect nectar from flowers.

Did You Know?
Tropical orchid bees have tongues that can measure twice the length of their own bodies. They need the long tongues to collect nectar from deep inside their namesake flowers, orchids.

their wings far too small to allow flight. The bumblebee proves that nature makes its own rules.

Digger bees are fast-flying, ground-nesting, velvety-furred bees that can grow to be as large as bumblebees. Although several thousand species exist worldwide, only 900 species can be found in the United States and Canada. Digger bees have odd nesting behavior. Although they are solitary bees, diggers seem to like company. Females build nests close to other females but not actually in a hive—a housing development of bees rather than an apartment building.

Carpenter bees seem to have the wrong name. Carpenters like to build with wood. Carpenter bees prefer boring holes and destroying wood. As large as bumblebees, these shiny black bees are extremely aggressive. There is no need to worry about the males, as they have no stingers, but females can inflict painful stings. The problem lies in telling the males from the females, since they pretty much look alike. Carpenter bees bore perfectly round holes into wood in which they lay their eggs. They prefer redwood, cedar, pine, or cypress because the wood is soft. A perfectly round, half-inch hole in window trim, fence posts, outdoor furniture, or a deck could be the new home of a

carpenter bee mother and her young. Warning: Do *not* poke a finger into the hole! An angry mother bee may be hiding inside.

Some bees like to provide a soft cushion for their young, and leafcutter bees fall into that category. Females bite off pieces of leaves to line their nests. Although these bees are ambitious in furnishing their nests, they are lazy in building them. Leafcutter bees would rather use someone else's home for theirs and are often found laying their eggs in mason wasp nests, bird nests, and even snail shells. Among the 140 species of leafcutter bees found in the

A carpenter bee looks out from its nest.

Did You Know?
More people in the United States die as a result of allergic reactions to bee stings each year than die from spider, snake, or scorpion bites.

United States, the most important may be the alfalfa leafcutter—an important grain pollinator.

Mason bees, the darlings of fruit growers everywhere, are another important species of pollinator. Anyone who eats an apple is enjoying the results of mason bees' efforts. Smaller than honeybees, mason bees can pollinate more flowers more efficiently than honeybees. Beekeepers devise homes for mason bees from blocks of wood with hundreds of holes bored in the surface. The mason bees move in, do a plastering job with a bit of mud, and happily spend their spring flitting from one apple blossom to the next.

Sweat bees get their name from their attraction to human body sweat—or rather the salts that form on the skin of humans while they sweat. More than 1,000 species of sweat bees live in the United States and Canada. Oddly, these bees do not like to follow a set behavior pattern. Some lay eggs in solitary nests, while other females share a community nest. Still other sweat bees share a hive populated by several active queens. Sweat bees may look a bit like flies, but watch out! Measuring a mere 3 to 10 millimeters (0.12 to 0.4 inches), sweat bees can deliver a powerful punch with their stingers.

Chapter Four

In Appreciation of Bees

A bee fell into a fast-running stream. The bee would have drowned, but a pigeon flying past plucked the bee from the water and saved it. The pigeon deposited the bee on a broad maple leaf. "Thank you, kind pigeon," the bee said. "Someday, I will repay you."

A few days later, the bee was busy collecting nectar from a field of clover. The bee spotted a hunter standing at the edge of the field. The bee watched as his friend the pigeon flew past. As the hunter raised his rifle, the bee hurried toward him. The bee stung the hunter just as the man was about to take his shot. The hunter's hand shook; the shot went wild. The pigeon flew on, unaware of his close call. In its own way, the bee repaid his debt.

This Ukrainian folktale is just one of many traditional stories in which the bee plays the hero. Bees appear in

myths, legends, fables, and folktales. Roman mythology said that Jupiter, the god of victory, was raised by both humans and honeybees.

Those are stories, but history notes the importance of bees, honey, and beeswax. Bees have been on Earth 10 to 20 million years longer than humans. Scientists believe that cave-dwelling

Who Said That?
As busie as a bee . . .
—*John Lyly, English author, in* Euphues and His England

Bees, such as the bumblebee, have become a part of many stories, myths, and legends.

human ancestors collected honey as long as five million years ago. Actual evidence of such activities appears in rock paintings in Europe and Asia that date back to about 13,000 BC. Beekeeping was common in ancient Egypt, Persia, China, Greece, and Rome.

Beeswax, a product of hives, has been commonly used for religious events for several thousand years. Offerings of wax accompanied births, marriages, and

Did You Know?
The biggest honey-producing countries in the world are China, the United States, Russia, Mexico, Argentina, and Canada.

Many people keep bees in human-made hives to collect the insects' honey.

deaths. Beeswax has also been used to embalm mummies and seal coffins.

BEE PRODUCTS AS MEDICINE

Bee therapy—the use of bee products in health care—goes as far back as ancient Egypt, Greece, and China. The Greek doctor Hippocrates often used bee venom to treat joint conditions. The method of using this venom leaves much to be desired. The bee's stinger is placed over the painful area, and the bee is encouraged to sting. The idea is that the venom eases the pain. There is no scientific proof that this works.

Bee products are commonly used in alternative medicine. Honey is a well-known antibacterial and antibiotic substance. It has been used to prevent infection in wounds. Bee pollen contains protein, minerals, and vitamins. Taken in pill form, bee pollen is supposed to increase energy and help people ward off allergy problems. Royal jelly is a milk-colored substance bees create to feed larvae that is taken by humans to fight fatigue, asthma, and lack of appetite. Royal jelly is commonly used in women's cosmetics, particularly for wrinkle-reducing face cream. As with bee venom, there is no scientific proof that bee pollen or royal jelly works in any of these situations.

Did You Know?
Honeybees are not native to the Americas. The first record of honeybees in the Western Hemisphere was in 1530 in South America when the Spanish brought them.

Chapter Five

Man and Bees

There are about 200 billion reasons for conserving bees. Yearly, $200 billion worth of crops grown worldwide depend on bees for pollination. There would be no strawberries or chocolate, no apples or oranges, and few fruits or vegetables or spices without bees. Worse, cattle, poultry, game birds, waterfowl, and game animals feed on plants, most of which are pollinated by bees. Without bees, those animals would have no food, and humans would have no meat, milk, cheese, or eggs. Bees are a vital link in the natural food chain, and essential in providing food for humans.

Beekeepers rent farmers hives full of bees when crop plants bloom. Not all these bees are honeybees. Bumblebees, for example, are commonly used in pollinating greenhouse tomatoes and strawberries. Mason bees are best for apple orchards. Alfalfa leafcutter bees are ideally suited to doing the job on grain crops. They can force the tiny alfalfa flowers to open and give up their pollen.

THREATS TO BEE POPULATIONS

The same threats to most insects also threaten bees: pesticides, habitat loss, habitat fragmentation, and non-native invaders. Pesticides are the biggest problem. A farmer sprays his or her crops to get rid of a specific insect. That poison soaks into the soil and when it rains, it is carried away from the farmer's fields through run off or washing through the soil. The poisoned water is sucked up

The existence of bees, such as this mason bee, is threatened by pesticides and other environmental dangers.

Did You Know?
Bees have an exceptional sense of smell—so fine that bees are being trained to sniff out land mines in war-torn countries. These mines are responsible for killing and maiming thousands. Thanks to bees, these dangerous weapons can be found and disarmed so they do not harm people in the future.

into other plants, and bees drink the poisoned nectar from those plants. It is a destructive cycle that ends up hurting the farmers, since reduced bee populations cannot do an efficient job of pollinating the crops.

Bees also face dangers from other bee species, including the Africanized bees shown here.

Did You Know?
Loss of honeybees and other pollinators may cost the United States up to $5.7 billion. Scientists estimate that 70 to 90 percent of wild bees have been lost in many states due to mites, harsh winters, pesticides, disease, and other problems.

Habitat loss and habitat fragmentation are similar problems. In one situation, meadows, wetlands, and open grasslands are plowed under to build housing, roads, or cities, or to create farmland. Bees that depend on fields of wildflowers cannot find sufficient nectar to support themselves and their young. Habitat fragmentation occurs when these same types of habitats are cut by roads, towns, or housing. Instead of one huge open field, plant growth is limited to small, separate plots. Bees must fly farther to collect less nectar and pollen.

Non-native invaders are insects, birds, or other species that do not come from a specific area and so compete with the animals that live there for resources. Occasionally, these could be other species of bees, such as Africanized bees. Humans need bees that produce honey and wax and pollinate crops. Species that destroy productive bees cause serious damage. Those species may be introduced intentionally by scientists experimenting with bee breeding, or they may arrive by accident in planes or on ships.

SOLUTIONS

Scientists are working toward finding new pollinators and safeguarding current bee populations. One solution is for

By starting a bee pasture, you can help bees—like this honeybee—survive.

beekeepers to domesticate other bee species as pollinators. For example, a beekeeper might create wood blocks for mason bees or leafcutter bees to use as homes.

Another good solution is growing bee pastures. This practice is similar to reforesting a pine forest by planting seedlings or reestablishing a wetland by getting rid of a dam. A bee pasture features a combination of annual and perennial plants that flower during different seasons. Nectar-rich flowers attract a great number of bee species. The more bees that flock to a field, the better the pollination and the greater the survival rate among bees.

It is better for a bee pasture to be one large area than several small plots separated by roads, towns, or housing developments. A permanent bee pasture will not only preserve bee species, it will lead to an increase in bee populations. It takes very little effort to plant and preserve a bee pasture, yet the end results are sizeable. Without humans, bees would survive quite well. Without bees, the human race would go hungry.

Glossary

abdomen (AB-doh-men) the lower section of an insect body

antennae (an-TEH-nee) sensory organs that stick out of an animal's head

facets (FAA-setz) the separate lenses that make up an insect's eye

fertilize (FUHR-tih-lyez) using sperm to make eggs capable of producing young

hibernate (HIGH-bur-nayt) to sleep through the winter

larva (LAHR-vuh) wormlike life stage of insects that develop into the pupa stage; the plural is *larvae* (LAHR-vee)

mandibles (MAN-dih-buhlz) the jaw parts of an insect's mouth

metamorphosis (meht-uh-MOR-foh-sis) a complete change in body form as an animal changes into an adult

ocelli (oh-SELL-eye) simple eyes that detect light

ommatidia (ahm-muh-TIHD-ee-uh) the visual facets of an insect eye

pheromone (FAIR-uh-mohn) chemical substances made by an animal to attract mates or to create trails for others of the species to follow

pollinating (PAHL-lih-nayt-ing) depositing pollen from one species of flower onto another flower of the same species

reproductive (ree-pro-DUK-tiv) having to do with producing young

solitary (SAHL-ih-tare-ee) to live alone or apart from others

thorax (THOR-aks) the middle body section of an insect, crustacean, or spider

For More Information

Watch It

David Attenborough's The Private Life of Plants, VHS. (Burbank, CA: BBC Video, 1995.)

National Geographic: The Swarm—India's Killer Bees, VHS. (Washington, DC: National Geographic Video, 2000.)

Read It

Kalman, Bobbie. *The Life Cycle of a Honeybee.* St. Catharine's, ON: Crabtree Publishing Company, 2004.

Markle, Sandra. *Outside and Inside Killer Bees.* New York: Walker Books for Young Readers, 2004.

Penny, Malcolm. *The Secret World of Bees.* Chicago: Raintree Publlishing, 2003.

Spilsbury, Richard, and Louise Spilsbury. *A Colony of Bees.* Chicago: Heinemann Library, 2004.

Look It Up

Visit our Web site for lots of links about bees:
http://www.childsworld.com/links

Note to Parents, Teachers, and Librarians: We routinely verify our Web links to make sure they are safe, active sites—so encourage your readers to check them out!

The Animal Kingdom
Where Do Bees Fit In?

Kingdom: Animal

Phylum: Arthropoda

Class: Insecta

Order: Hymenoptera

Species: 25,000 species of bees

Relatives: Wasps and ants

Index

About the Author

Sophie Lockwood is a former teacher and a longtime writer. She writes textbooks, newspaper articles, and magazine articles. Sophie enjoys writing about animals and their habits. The most interesting part of her research, Sophie says, is learning how scientists apply their knowledge to save endangered species. She lives with her husband in the foothills of the Blue Ridge Mountains.